CHANGING CHICHESTER

CHANGING CHICHESTER

BERNARD PRICE

Phillimore

1982

Published by
PHILLIMORE & CO. LTD.
London and Chichester

Head Office: Shopwyke Hall,
Chichester, Sussex, England

ISBN 0 85033 430 6

*This book, together with its companion volumes
'Bygone Chichester' and 'Chichester: The Valiant Years',
is dedicated by the author
to all who love Chichester,
past, present and future*

Printed and bound in Great Britain by
BILLING & SONS LTD
Guildford, London, Oxford, Worcester

LIST OF ILLUSTRATIONS

INTRODUCTION

This book completes the trilogy of Chichester volumes that I began in 1975. More than seven years in search of photographs and drawings of the city has, for me, been sheer delight. Now I can but hope that these three books containing, together with documents, over 650 illustrations, will bring pleasure, interest and much food for thought. The photographs span more than a century, from 1861 to the late 1960s. The watercolours of Chichester tradesmen date from 1850.

Obviously, the task of deciding what and what not to include has been difficult. In many cases the problem was resolved for me by the material available and the condition of it. I have set out to reflect change in building, street scenes, and social conditions, and to portray as many local people as possible. It would not have been practical to have attempted to include all aspects of local life, the activities of clubs, societies, and other bodies. They will, I trust, maintain their own careful records.

Today, with so many simple, yet excellent, cameras available, it should be possible for all families to maintain photographic records. In 1981 Dr. Roy Strong, Director of the Victoria and Albert Museum, also urged that such material should be kept. Not only the family snap, but the interiors of rooms and their contents, alterations to the house, changes made in the garden, and family transport. Memories are often very short and are easily distorted. Family albums should always bear the name and address of the family concerned, and all photographs need to be identified and dated.

What has become very clear to me in recent years is that one man's treasure is often but mere rubbish to another. The result has been the destruction of thousands of potentially important photographs simply because people who have inherited them have been unable to identify them. A sense of history is an invaluable gift indeed.

Change is very much the theme of this book for, since 1945, Chichester has seen change on a scale not seen before in centuries. The two main factors involved have been motor transport and population. The old city within the Roman walls has grown slowly, the product of hundreds of years in an area not much more than a hundred acres.

The Georgian and domestic nature of Chichester is no longer what it was, and the massive development of County Hall is, in my view, misplaced. The street scenes in all historic cities have now come to be influenced by supermarket buildings, and new methods of packaging which have, in turn, influenced window displays.

In Chichester whole areas of artisan cottages have disappeared, at Tower Street, Chapel Street and, of course, Somerstown. Most of these late Georgian cottages were in urgent need of repair and restoration. Low rents were being paid for these tenanted cottages and very few local landlords were prepared to spend the money required to put them in order.

In Somerstown, as tenants were rehoused, so increasing numbers of houses became derelict. More than a decade passed before redevelopment. It is now far too late to argue, but restoration rather than devastation might well have been the more wise and character-retaining course. In the City Council Chamber strong arguments were also being put forward for the demolition of the North Walls, which, thankfully, were defeated. Meanwhile, the upper floors of many Chichester shops remained empty and deteriorating, their owners or tenants now living outside the city, a movement that had already begun to take place late in the 19th century.

Such events created interest, concern, and controversy among local people, and the voices of citizens came increasingly to be heard over matters of planning. Some of the criticism was, and is, negative, but as Lord Tennyson, chairman of the London Appreciation Society, said in March 1982: 'The two villains are self interest and the planner who "sees a need".'

On Monday 17 June 1974, a town meeting was held in Chichester Cathedral where views on changes in Chichester were put forward by a panel of speakers, of whom I was one, to an audience of some 2,000 people. Christopher Fry had written a sonnet for the Chichester Society and it was spoken at the meeting by Irene Worth. With Christopher Fry's kind permission, I reproduce it here.

> What can be said of the spoiler of cities?—
> The perpetrator of a thousand pities,
> Who, like the drunken surgeon with a knife,
> Thinking to cure, cuts out the life—
> Who banishes, with gesture brief and graphic,
> Whatever charm disturbs the flow of traffic—
> Whose lips compress, whose cardiac centre hardens
> To see a city's heart alight with hidden gardens?
> What can be said of him who sees no stature
> In the uniqueness of a city's nature?
> 'Alas' is easily said; but no sigh pays the cost
> Of dignity destroyed and beauty lost.
> And nothing then can reinstate
> A city that we cared about too late.

Christopher Fry

The following year I wrote and presented a half-hour television documentary for the B.B.C., to mark the 900th Anniversary of Chichester Cathedral. The following lines formed the final 90 seconds of commentary:

'Chichester has never been afraid of innovation, and the market cross itself is a symbol of change, but certain values are timeless. The Georgian sense of enclosure in St Martin's Square, or the intense architectural satisfaction of the meandering Lion Street, is all part of Chichester's character. These are not grand houses but they do put buoyancy into the spirit, which can seldom be said of concrete, and there is a sense of privacy forever denied to plate glass. Fine things of all periods establish a harmony of their own, but too many buildings in Chichester are now striking the wrong note, the standard cash-till money platform of the chain store just isn't good enough.

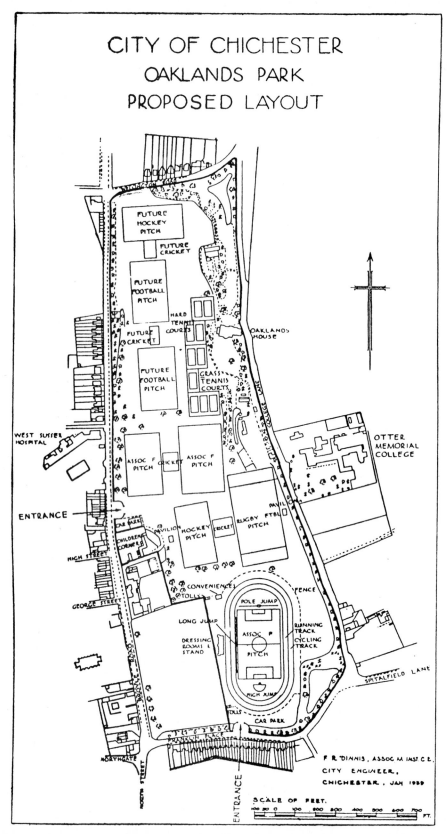

1. Plan of Proposed layout of Oaklands Park.

'Over the past year the city has heard the drum-beat of public opinion, shocked by demolition and a Post Office block that is totally alien in character. I believe that all new buildings should be on the domestic scale Chichester was built for, not administrative factories or bleak barns for telephone switch gear, red brick or not.

'The lion above the Council Chamber has had its teeth eroded, due to weather and local government re-organisation, yet as a hall-mark it could hardly be more apt. For Chichester is unashamedly English; the City and Cathedral consecrated by time, yet ever at risk of complacency that so often takes for granted that which is irreplaceable.'

In view of the growing enthusiasm for the establishment of a sports complex in Chichester, some people may find the following little-known document, published by the city in August 1939, of particular interest (see opposite for plan of layout):

'The City Council, under the powers conferred by the Physical Training and Recreation Act, 1937, have recently acquired the property known as Oaklands Park (comprising some 43 acres) at a cost of £13,000 for the purpose of a sports centre. The estate is beautifully timbered and situate only five minutes' walk from the Market Cross, the centre of the City.

'In consultation with the newly-formed Chichester Sports Clubs' Association and with the advice of the National Playing Fields Association the lay-out plan reproduced on the opposite page has been prepared by the City Engineer and Surveyor.

'The following recreational facilities are proposed, namely: A Sports Stadium, with seating accommodation for 400 people, comprising a football pitch, running track, cycling track, high jump, long jump, pole vault, dressing room and conveniences; a rugby pitch and pavilion, two football pitches, eight grass tennis courts, four hard tennis courts, children's corner, two cricket pitches and a netball pitch. A portion of the site will be reserved for camping.

'The lay-out, estimated to cost a further £11,600 (the greater part of which will be met by way of grant from the Board of Education through the National Fitness Council), recognises to a very large extent the wide variety of the demands for physical recreation; indeed it is not too much to say that provision has been made for almost every taste.

'The proposed sports centre will provide the City and this part of West Sussex with first class up-to-date recreational facilities, and it is confidently expected that Chichester will possess one of the finest sports centres in the South of England, and the Council look to the public for their support and co-operation . . .'.

The declaration of War a month later would have pigeonholed all thoughts of a sports stadium.

Many interesting people came to Chichester between the wars, the most surprising, perhaps, being Mahatma Gandhi. The Indian leader arrived in the city on 10 October 1931, staying with Bishop Bell at the Bishop's Palace. Gandhi walked along part of the tow-path of Chichester Canal each morning, and visited Bognor Regis to see his old friend C. P. Scott, then editor of the *Manchester Guardian*.

Chichester has had a long association with speed as the photographs will show. The Duke of Richmond and Gordon was a successful racing driver in the days of Brooklands, as well as being a fine pilot. In 1914 South Harting Hill was the centre for drivers whose sport was hill-climbing.

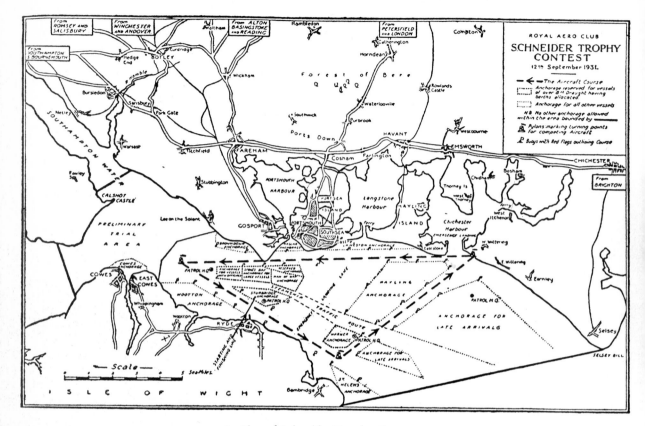

2. Plan of Schneider Trophy Contest.

Sir Henry Royce came to live at West Wittering, and photographs of him at that time are included in this book. In 1931 when the Schneider Trophy Contest was won outright for Great Britain, it also brought the world's speed record with it. From his home Sir Henry was able to time the aircraft as it turned over East Head.

The latest addition to Chichester's attractions is the opening of Pallant House Gallery, a building that has undergone much change. It will add a whole new dimension to the city, for Chichester was made well aware of its lack of a gallery when the exhibition 'The Painter and the Stage' was held at 43 North Street in 1962.

So Chichester moves on, hopefully, as I trust it always will, changing, and being guided by people who love her. I also look forward to the day when buildings, or sites in the city, carry plaques to record historic events or people; which can only add interest for the visitor, and remind residents of their precious inheritance.

BERNARD PRICE

3. The Dining Rooms of George Benham, North Street, were a popular local meeting place. As may be seen from the advertisements Mr. Benham was also a beer retailer. For many years a brandy barrel hung in his window, it was one of a number that had been discovered in caves in Brandy Hole Lane. Mr. G. Parsons writing to the local press early this century states: 'The cave from which Brandy Hole Lane, Chichester, obtains its name is, or was, in the lane close to the Midhurst railway line. The entrance to it until the railway line was built, was open, I believe it was filled in during the building of the road bridge; it was an apartment of considerable size, with a passageway leading north'. The above photograph depicts John Benham sometime between 1900 and 1914.

4. (*left*) The firm of Frederick Pennicott & Co., of Oving Road, were well known grocers through several generations.

5. (*centre*) The Pennicott's motor delivery van is typical of such early vehicles that gave good service over many years.

6. (*below*) The Voke family of Chichester were renowned locally as bakers and confectioners, a business previously pursued by George Mant of North Street.

7. (*top*) Tradesmen's vehicles were always maintained with great pride, a fact clearly evident from this photograph.

8. (*above*) H. J. Voke & Sons bakery and tea-gardens in the Hornet, were on the grand scale, sufficiently extensive to deal with almost any local occasion, and a large staff was maintained. (Plate 140 in *Bygone Chichester* shows the scene in the Hornet on the opening day).

9. (*opposite above*) This superb photograph of an early Chichester delivery vehicle reveals many fascinating details. Note, for example, the fine pair of brass coach-lamps and the bulb operated horn.

10. (*opposite below*) The horse-drawn van of William Kimbell on parade in Chichester, *c.* 1920. The horses are particularly fine animals and beautifully turned out.

11. (*right*) At the same Van-Horse Parade the rag-and-bone men were also ready to show off their wagon and skills with heavy horses.

12. (*below*) The exquisite examples of the cabinet makers craft shown here were made by members of the Peat family, from Samuel born in 1734, to Frederick in 1851. (Plate 33 in *Bygone Chichester*, depicts Samuel Peat, 1814-1899. He was highly commended for a cylinder-fall writing desk at the Great Exhibition of 1851).

13. (*left*) Teddy Game of Broyle Road, drawing his final loaf, Somerstown's last baker.

14. (*below left*) The shop of Frank Tees, 28 Oving Road. Mr. Tees was a general dealer but specialised in oil and hardware, cycle accessories and second-hand clothing; he also did considerable business in the hiring of bicycle trailers.

15. (*opposite*) Bull's Ltd. of North Street, dealt in china and glass, hardware, toys and fancy goods. This bill of October 1927 is for a child's gramophone (*see* Plate 17). Costing less than 25p., this instrument remains in good order today.

16. (*far right*) Alfred Reynolds premises at 84 East Street. Late 1920s. By 1931 the firm had changed its name to Guy Reynolds, Gents' Outfitter. Later the firm moved to its present location at 77 North Street.

17. (*opposite below*) Child's gramophone as mentioned in Caption No. 15.

Lewis' Motor Outings.

OUT AND HOME FROM
BOGNOR AND
CHICHESTER.

Programme
OF
WHOLE DAY AND HALF-DAY TOURS.

For times and descriptive illustrated particulars of each Tour, see within.

Book Seats at—

GARAGE, LONGFORD ROAD, BOGNOR. Tel. 89.

BOOKING CLERK AT PIER CHAR-A-BANC STAND and

SOUTHGATE, CHICHESTER. Tel. 153.

All Char-a-banes start from the Pier, Bognor, and Corn Exchange, Chichester.

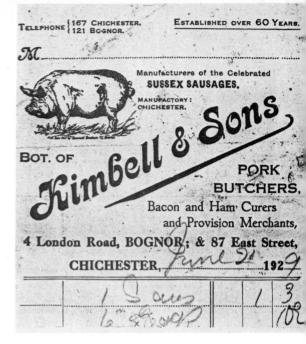

TELEPHONE { 167 CHICHESTER. 121 BOGNOR. ESTABLISHED OVER 60 YEARS.

M_____

Manufacturers of the Celebrated
SUSSEX SAUSAGES.

MANUFACTORY: CHICHESTER.

BOT. OF

Kimbell & Sons

PORK BUTCHERS,
Bacon and Ham Curers
and Provision Merchants,

4 London Road, BOGNOR; & 87 East Street,

CHICHESTER, _June 21_ 1929

19. (*above*) A bill head of Messrs Kimbell & Sons, 1929, famous for their Sussex sausages. (*see also,* *Chichester, the Valiant Years,* Plate 77).

18a & 18b. (*above & below*) Messrs Lewis of Chichester and Bognor, carried on the business of furniture removal, but they also became tour operators as this advertisement and photograph of their char-a-banc reveals.

LEWIS' TOURING CAR.   Unequalled for Comfort.

20. (*above*) War workers engaged in the manufacture of aircraft fuel tanks pose for the camera at the rear of Wadham's garage, Southgate. Note Mr. Charlie Newell (*Back row, left*), later Mayor and Freeman of Chichester.

21. (*right*) The historic letter received by Shippams from Captain Scott, RN, while leading the ill-fated but heroic British Antarctic expedition to the South Pole, 1910-1912. In more recent times, Captain Scott's son, Sir Peter Scott, visited his father's base camp and found tins of sausages still in perfect condition!

(For Queen Mary's visit to Shippams Ltd., see *Bygone Chichester*, Plates 12, 13 & 14).

Winter Quarters.
October 20th 1911

Dear Sir

It was originally intended that the goods which you supplied to the Expedition should be used entirely on the ship but owing to their excellent quality a considerable quantity was landed for use at our Winter Station

I have much pleasure in informing you that this supply has remained in good condition and has been highly appreciated

Your faithfully

R Scott

C. Shippam
Chichester

22. Many small businesses have gone from Chichester, including Adams the butchers at 67 East Street.

23. The late Mr. Nelson Fowler, over-looker and wool buyer for the old Chichester firm of Ebenezer Prior Ltd., wool staplers and wool merchants. Their Tower Street premises occupied a site opposite the county library building. (Other photographs concerning Chichester's wool merchants are to be found in *Chichester, the Valiant Years*).

PHARMACEUTICAL SOCIETY OF GREAT BRITAIN,

17, BLOOMSBURY SQUARE, W.C.

PHARMACY ACT, 1868 (DATED 31ST JULY).

Received this 11th day of November, 1868, of

Mr. Edward Baker

of East Gate Chichester

Sussex

the DECLARATIONS according to Schedules C and D of the above Act, for Registration as a "Chemist and Druggist."

Registrar.

24. (*above*) On his return from the Crimean War, Edward Baker became the chemist and druggist at Eastgate Square. (*See Bygone Chichester* Plate 32).

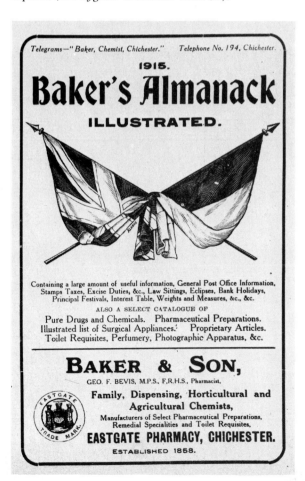

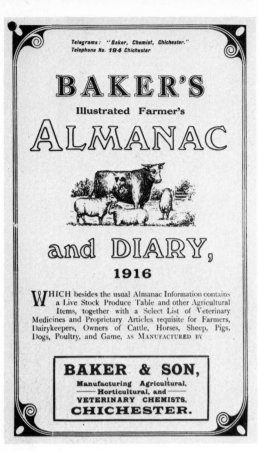

Valuable and Excellent Family Medicine.

WRIGHT'S

DANDELION & RHUBARB PILLS

AN FFFECTUAL REMEDY for Liver Affections, Diseases of the Stomach and Bowels, Indigestion, Habitual Costiveness, Bilious and Sick Head-ache. Heartburn, Wind, Spasms, Loss of Appetite, Nervous Depression, Fulness at Pit of Stomach, Jaundice, Foul Breath, Giddiness in the Head, and Dizziness of the Eyes, &c., &c.

During a period of over quarter of a century these celebrated Pills have stood the test, being used most extensively as a family medicine by thousands of families residing in Chichester and its neighbourhood, who have always found them a simple and safe remedy, and one needful to be always kept at hand. Those who may not have hitherto proved their efficacy will do well to give them a trial.

5. 26, 27, 28 & 29. (*previous pages*) The previous five plates of advertisements demonstrate the remarkable range
f services and preparations provided by this firm, from the extermination of bunions to the cure-all of 'Wrights
andelion and rhubarb pills'.

30. (*above*) Mr. George Bevis M.P.S. stands at the side of his window display commemorating '100 years of pharmacy' 1858-1958. The pharmacy had been established by Robert Wright of whom little is known, but it was he who sold the business to Edward Baker, ex-hospital sergeant and hero of the Crimea. In 1872 Baker's son, Samuel, qualified as a chemist and also carried out dentistry. Mr. Bevis retired from business in 1981.

31. (*left*) Charge & Co. were one of Chichester's best known drapers and occupied the site at the junction of East and South Streets; this photograph was taken from beneath the city Cross. The firm was established in the city for more than 200 years, the Post Office directory of a century ago described the firm as 'linen draper, silk mercer and clothier'. The building was acquired by Midland Bank in 1968-69 and developed by them in 1970-71.

This unique series of water-colour portraits provides a rare view of tradesmen and other personalities in mid-Victorian Chichester.

32. Edward Habin, harness-maker, saddler and corn merchant, The Hornet

33. Ralph Horton, innkeeper, The *Swan*, East Street.

34. Unidentified, possibly a chemist.

35. John Kemp, grocer, tallow-chandler and provision merchant, East Street

36. Henry Newland,
solicitor,
North Pallant.

37. Thomas Shipley,
carver and gilder,
North Street.

38. Edward Combes,
wine and spirit merchant,
East and West Street.

39. Robert Pasco,
tailor,
East Street.

How do you do George

40. Count Fogden,
clerk to William Duke, solicitor,
North Pallant.

41. George Field,
gentleman,
Southgate.

42 James Gates,
butcher,
East Street.

43. Barnard Hyams,
jeweller,
West Street.

44. Samuel Merricks,
grocer,
South Street.

45 Mr. Ben Brown,
town crier.

46. William Beatson,
fishmonger and poulterer,
North Street.

47. Drummond Gray,
carver and gilder,
East Street.

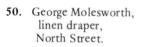

Order! Mr Gadd is on his legs

48. Alexander Davis,
ironmonger,
East Street.

49. Mr. Gadd,
grocer.

50. George Molesworth,
linen draper,
North Street.

51. George Gambling,
saddler,
South Street.

52. Thomas Kitson,
stonemason,
Lion Street.

53. Edward Collins,
linen draper,
North Street.

54. Joe Barber,
grocer,
Cavendish Street.

55. Edward Titchener,
Clerk of the Peace.

56. Fred Weller,
rate collector,
South Street.

57. John Hewett,
baker,
South Street.

59. John Lush White,
auctioneer, estate agent, cabinet maker,
North Street.

58. 'Kidney' Harris.

60. John Austin.

61. Old Farr.

62. Mr. Parr,
West Street.

63. James Gale,
fruiterer,
West Street.

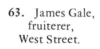

64. Mr. Green,

65. George Tully Dendy,
corn merchant,
North Street.

66. Unidentified.

67. Sergeant Lambert.

68. (*above*) This superb photograph probably dates from between 1870 and 1885. The name on the corner shop, to the left of the Cross, is Glover and refers to Mary Ann Glover, stationer. Wheel tracks can be clearly seen in the unmade surface of West Street.

MARKET CROSS, CHICHESTER. 1641.31

69. (*opposite above*) A flock of sheep make their way around the Cross, late 19th century. Cattle were still driven through the city until the late 1940s.

70. (*opposite below*) This interesting picture shows how the corner shop referred to in Plate 68 has now changed hands and is occupied by Barrett, stationer, newsagent, book-binder and artists colourman. To the right of the Cross is Mr. Panchen's hairdressing salon.

71. A stylised engraving of the mid-19th century that does succeed in giving something of the atmosphere of the period.

72. A charming photograph taken, *c.* 1920, from the theological college at Westgate. The many-angled roofs and chimney pots are a delight to the eye.

73. No other photograph the author has seen so far conveys the charm of the old Eastgate Square so well as this picture. In the foreground is a cobbled crossing, and the building on the left is the Eastgate Hand Laundry.

74. (*above*) Chichester Corn Exchange, with its impressive iron columns, was built in 1833 in order to deal with the growing trade in wheat and barley. It is a monument to the skill and knowledge of the local farmers and millers of the 19th century.

75a,b,c & d. (*right & below*) Here we see the title page for the rules of management for the Corn Exchange published in 1832, a most rare pamphlet. Particularly interesting is the list of shareholders, in which so many well known local names are listed. Part of the building was still used as a corn exchange until the 1960s.

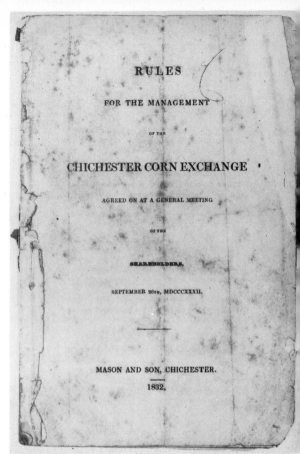

RULES

FOR THE MANAGEMENT

OF THE

CHICHESTER CORN EXCHANGE

AGREED ON AT A GENERAL MEETING

OF THE

SHAREHOLDERS,

SEPTEMBER 26TH, MDCCCXXXII.

MASON AND SON, CHICHESTER.
1832.

LIST
OF
SHAREHOLDERS.

NAMES.	RESIDENCE.	No. of Shares.
Adames, John, Jun.	Pagham	4
Agate, William	New Fishbourne	2
Barbut, Rev. Stephen	Chichester	2
Bayley, George	Eartham	2
Bennett, Edward	Bosham	2
Bennett, Thomas	Bosham	4
Biffin, James	Chichester	1
Biffin, John	Chichester	1
Biffin, Charles	Chichester	1
Binstead, Benjamin	Chichester	1
Caffin, Benjamin	Chichester	2
Caffin, James	Chichester	2
Cobden, Hugh	Hulnaker	4
Cogan, Stephen	Funtington	4
Combes, William	Chichester	5
Cottrell, John	Chichester	2

12

Duke, Charles	Funtington	5
Farndell, Stephen	Bosham	10
Farndell, Joseph	Dell Quay	10
Field, William	Rumboldswhyke	1
Field, William R.	Rumboldswhyke	1
Florance, Edmund	St. Pancrass	1
Florance, William A.	St. Pancrass	1
Freeland, Henry	Appledram	4
Gatehouse, George	Chichester	1
Gatehouse, Charles	Chichester	1
Gatehouse, John	Chichester	1
Gatehouse, Richard	Chichester	1
Gibbs, William	Itchenor	4
Goringe, William	Kingston	2
Gruggen, William	Chichester	3
Hack, James	Chichester	10
Halsted, Thomas	Woodcote	10
Halsted, Henry	Merston	4
Hardwicke,	Goodwood	4
Hayllar, James Parvin	Hornet	4
Hayllar, Thomas	St. Pancrass	4
Henty, George	Chichester	10
Henty, Robert	Chichester	10
Henty, Samuel		4
Henty, William	East Lavant	2
Hodge, John Voyce	Chichester	4
Hodge, William	Chichester	2
Ide, John	West Wittering	4
Johnson, John James	Chichester	4
Leggatt, George	West Hampnett	4

13

Owens, Richard	Chichester	1
Pitt, William	St. Pancrass	1
Powell, James	Chichester	2
Raper Robert	Chichester	1
Reynolds, Charles	Chichester	3
Robins, William	Chichester	2
Robins, Richard Brazier	East Lavant	2
Rusbridger, John	Goodwood	8
Rusbridger, John, Jun.	Goodwood	1
Rusbridger, George	Goodwood	1
Sadler, Henry	Mid-Lavant	4
Sherwood, John	Chichester	5
Shippam, William	Chichester	4
Slater, John Dorrill	Chichester	1
Smith, William	Chichester	2
Souter, George	Boxgrove	4
Stich, William	Chichester	2
Voke, James	Chichester	1
White, Thomas	Chichester	1
Winter, Barnard John	Chichester	4
Woods, John, Esq.	Chilgrove	10
Woods, Edmund, Esq.	Shopwyke	10
Young, William	West Stoke	2

76a & b. (*right*) That the Corn Exchange should eventually become a cinema was not such an unlikely progression as it sounds. From the early years of the century it had been a centre for drama. Mrs. James from West Dean House took part in several productions at the Exchange, so too did Bransby Williams. Local amateur talent made it a centre of entertainment, with many of the audience sitting on corn bins. The golden period of cinema activity came between 1930 and the early 1950s. The advertisements shown here are evocative of the period and its economics. Today the building faces further change.

EXCHANGE
THEATRE
CHICHESTER

'Phone 407

MATINEE DAILY at 2.30

REDUCED PRICES—

7d. - 9d. - 1/3

EVENINGS CONTINUOUS
From 6 p.m. (*Doors Open* 5.30)

7d. — 9d.
1/3 — 1/6 — 2/-

*Children at reduced prices, except
Saturdays and Bank Holidays.*

Always a Good Show!

Sidney C. Lacey
——— LIMITED ———

85, East Street,
CHICHESTER

THE SUSSEX STATIONERS

*Printers, Booksellers, High
Class Leather and Electro
Plated Articles.*

Willis, Printers, Chichester [*See Over*

**Features for
SEPT., 1932**

Thursday, Sept. 1st—*For 3 days*
Gordon Harker
Edgar Wallace's Thriller
THE FRIGHTENED LADY.

Monday, Sept. 5th—*All the Week.*
England's Greatest Musical
Comedy Star
JACK BUCHANAN
GOOD NIGHT VIENNA

Monday, Sept. 12th—*All the Week*
TOM WALLS   RALPH LYNN
Roy Fox and His Band
A NIGHT LIKE THIS
The Best of them all.

Monday, Sept. 19th—*3 days* only
GEORGE ARLISS
in his Masterpiece
THE SILENT VOICE.

Thursday, Sept. 22nd—*For 3 days*
GENE GERRARD
Brother Alfred
Hilarious Comedy by
P. G. WODEHOUSE

Monday, Sept. 26th—*For 3 days.*
Charles "Chic" Sale
THE EXPERT
Also—Nora Swinburne in
Voice Said Goodnight
Mickey Mouse Cartoon.

Thursday, Sept. 29th—*For 3 days*
Marion Davies
Clarke Gable
POLLY OF THE CIRCUS

77. (*below*) On 23 September 1897, a devastating fire broke out in the East Street premises formerly used as the *Swan* Hotel and Posting House, but for many years subsequent to that they were occupied by Samuel Edney, house furnisher, and Samuel Crosbie, tailor. This disaster was always referred to as 'Edney's fire'.

78. A beautiful photograph of a cathedral city, its quiet unbroken by modern machines, and a life lived at pedestrian pace or at the speed of a trotting horse. Note the gates on John Edes' house, (left) then a private residence, and the handsome lamps of the gaslit street.

79. (*above*) The scene at Southgate for the laying of memorial stones of the new Wesleyan chapel, on Friday 31 March 1876. Only two years earlier a Chichester primitive methodist, Mrs. Sarah Clark, standing with her husband and another preacher, had been killed by a bottle thrown by a hostile member of their audience during an open-air meeting at Somerstown.

80. (*left*) The Rev. Waterhouse, the first minister of the Methodist church at Southgate.

81. (*opposite*) A glimpse through the Eastgate arch built for Coronation day, 1911. (For a view looking westward through this archway, see *Bygone Chichester,* Plate 27).

82. (*above*) This fine mansion was built for Henry 'Lisbon' Peckham, a wine importer of the early 18th century. For many years it served as local government office accommodation and was known locally as 'The Dodo House', due to the stone birds on the entrance gate which are, in fact, ostriches from the Peckham Crest. Since May 1982 the building has re-opened as Chichester's first public art gallery.

83. (*left*) The fine premises at 30 East Street, of the old Capital and Counties Bank Ltd., established in 1834. Later this building was re-developed as Messrs David Greig, provision merchants, who traded in Chichester for many years.

84. (*above*) This Norman door in the south-west tower of the cathedral was recently re-opened after being sealed for many years.

85. (*above right*) An excellent view of St Peter's 14th century church, North Street, now demolished.

86. (*right*) East Street crowds on Coronation day 1902.

Chichester Cathedral, West Front from Bishop's Garden

87. The rarely appreciated view of the west front of the Cathedral as seen from the Bishop's garden.

88. In 1959 the Dean and Chapter purchased the Royal Chantry, it had been out of their possession since 1549. Its front door opens into the cathedral cloister, and the garden entrance gives on to the close.

89. North Walls viewed from the west.

90. (*left*) Houses and stables in Tower Street. The cottage with the white sign flush to the wall above its door indicates the 'March Charity' and soup kitchen, *c.* 1900.

91. (*below left*) An elegant looking Tower Street viewed from North Walls.

92. (*below*) Tower Street viewed from the bell tower, *c.* 1920.

93 & 94. As preceding pictures have shown, Tower Street until the 1950s was a most interesting mixture of building styles, a few substantial houses, artisan cottages, a school, a public house and the wool warehouses of Ebenezer Prior Ltd. Plate 93 shows this street in its final days. Plate 94 is filled with the haunted look of dereliction.

95. (*below*) Only the pavement remains, beyond the garden walls is Chapel Street, most of which has also been demolished.

96. (*opposite*) The Market Cross, *c.* 1501. This drawing is from the pencil and brush of Eric Gill, 1882-1940. Gill made this drawing and many others while living in Chichester during his early teens. This work, probably his best of that period, has all the spirit of a renaissance drawing. In recent years the Cross has undergone extensive restoration.

Market Cross Chichester

E. A. Grier

97. (*left*) The Butter Market, North Street, prior to i[t]
alteration and adaption in 1954.

98. (*below left*) A romantic and nostalgic glimpse of
the old tree-filled gardens between North Walls and
the cathedral.

99. (*below*) A close-up view of the old cannon shown
above left. Once they protected the buildings from the
wheels of coaches that used this entrance to gain access
to the *Swan* Hotel, East Street. The cannon were removed
from Chichester when the site was developed.

100. (*left*) South Street begins to move firmly into the 20th century. At No. 55, the cycle and motor works, they were advertising garage facilities, and not a motor vehicle in sight!

101. (*below*) A steamroller causes concern at the Cross, *c.* 1935.

102. The island site at Eastgate Square totally cleared in readiness for rebuilding the *Unicorn* by Messrs Henty & Constable, the Chichester brewers. (See also *Chichester, the Valiant Years,* Plate 98).

103. (*above*) The meeting place of the Plymouth Brethren, in a first floor room in Crane Street; during the 1930s they moved to premises in Chapel Street.

104. (*left*) St John's church, St John's Street, decorated for Harvest Festival. This most interesting building was built to the design of James Elms in 1812.

105. Chichester Old Bank issued its own bank notes as did most banks in towns of any importance. The bank was situated at No. 11 East Street, later to become the Central Boot Co. These premises were purchased by Lloyds Bank and incorporated into their larger branch.

106. Cheques issued by the London & County Bank, at 94 East Street. Later it became the London & Midland Bank.

107. John Leng & Sons were cabinet makers, furniture and antique dealers, at the junction of Eastgate Square and St Pancras. The firm closed in the 1960s and the site was redeveloped. (For a further photograph, see *Bygone Chichester*, Plate 55).

108. (*below left*) Mrs. Morgan's tiny grocery and provision store at the junction of Chapel Street and Orchard Street.

109. (*below right*) Part of South Street that has drastically changed. In this picture the Odeon cinema was showing *The Browning Version*, Maison Max the hairdresser had closed and the old Post Office sorting office was still in use early in the 1950s.

10. (*right*) This Georgian house adjoining the North Walls was replaced with a modern building. It was the premises of T. C. Daniels, electrical engineers.

11. (*below*) These stone steps came to light after an 18th-century building had been pulled down and digging was begun for a garage's petrol storage tank. Found only a few inches below the surface, they are part of the Roman North Gate and were the first clue to the precise position of any of the city's four gates.

112. (*above*) St Peter's House, North Street, shored-up with timbers after the demolition of the church of St Peter the Less in 1957.

113. (*right*) Garland's grocery shop at Eastgate, the oldest in Britain, demolished in 1964. (For a fine photograph of its interior, see *Bygone Chichester,* Plate 130).

114. (*left*) After a crack had appeared in the front wall, the old shop was demolished with almost indecent haste, the site remaining derelict for years.

115. (*below*) The old west entrance to the city, or 'bottle-neck' as it was so often termed. Older residents will remember the little shop of Mr. and Mrs. Henstridge. During these demolitions, Eric Gill's house was also destroyed and in the process the enclosed Georgian character of Westgate was lost.

CHICHESTER FROM THE CANAL. 5788 J.V.

116. (*above left*) This leaping dolphin carved in wood over Bosun's Locker in St Martin's Street is the work of John Skelton, Eric Gill's nephew and last apprentice.

117. (*left*) The scene in West Street, c. 1946.

18. The Chichester canal was much favoured as a subject by Victorian photographers. This view constantly appears ut this photograph is remarkable for its detail of the gasworks buildings, and the sense of dominance created by the athedral.

119. Photographs are unique in their manner of capturing a moment in time. Priory Park could hardly appear more Victorian than it does here, the feeling of a glorious afternoon that will never end, and that all is well with the world.

120. This picture of the choir building of The Grey Friars was probably taken on the same day as the previous photograph. The fine old tree and the seat that girded it were not removed until after World War II.

121. West Street was always the most residential of the four main streets and it continues to hold much interesting architectural detail and building styles. This view of the Prebendal School probably dates from the late 1940s.

122. The author took this photograph in 1954, prior to the construction of the Avenue de Chartres. At that time the city was still unique in Britain in having agricultural land with grazing cattle reaching to the city walls. This quality of rural farmland was quite different to the sense of public open space that prevails today.

123. (*above*) These cottages in Farr's Court, St Pancras, were demolished long ago. Their charm was captured for posterity by the brush of Harry Wimhurst who drew many interesting corners at the beginning of the century.

124. (*right*) The old 'crooked S' or 'Shambles Alley' leading into North Street, again by H. Wimhurst, dated 1905.

125. Dark cloister at the rear of St Faith's continues
to preserve its unassuming quiet charm.
H. Wimhurst, 1900.

126. Cottages in Priory Lane, now redeveloped
as part of the Northgate garage. Drawn in pen and
ink by H. Wimhurst.

127. Near Spitalfield Lane, an area much developed since 1945. A plaque on this cottage marks the site of the lazar or leper hospital of St James and St Mary Magdalene, probably founded early in the 12th century.

The heart of Somerstown consisted of three streets in the form of an H. George Street and High Street linked by Cross Street. The two main streets ran from Broyle Road to St Paul's Road where they faced Parchment Street and Washington Street.

128.   Soon after the opening of the Chichester Festival Theatre, these lovely old cottages, Lennox Place, Broyle Road, overlooking the theatre and Oaklands Park, were demolished.

129.   Some of the mellow roofscapes of Somerstown as seen from an upper window of the old vicarage.

130. George Street looking east. A variety of roof levels, door cases, tile hanging and a varied building line, provides interest to the eye and the harmony of period. Cross Street is on the left.

131. A long view of the north side of George Street.

132. Fine houses in High Street.

133. High Street looking east to the Festival Theatre. Some of the cottages seen here are of a later period, others heavily restored.

134. (*right*) A number of public houses were situated in Somerstown. This photograph shows the *Spotted Cow* and adjoining buildings.

135. (*below*) Plate glass was slow to make inroads here, hence the survival of fine astragal window frames of the late Georgian period.

136. (*above*) The builders move in! The old tiles, door knockers, insurance plaques, iron footscrapers and doorcases disappear forever.

137. (*below*) In the view of many people, the ignoble end to Somerstown meant the passing of an asset of great potential value.

George Street - Chichester

Victor Slaymaker
1967

138. A few outposts remain. A drawing by Victor Slaymaker, 1967.

139. After years as a derelict site new building at last begins. The new homes are most comfortable and many offer fine prospects of the city from their windows. The question, however, that will always be raised, is, would not a resolute decision to restore old Somerstown have added far more to the character and nature of the city?

40. (*above*) Libraries have played an invaluable role in life and learning in Chichester. The first reference to the cathedral library was made in the 12th century. Ever since then the city has been associated with books and fine printers. Shown above is a rare and handsome bookplate of 1794.

41. (*right*) Presentation from the Chichester Book Society in 1841.

42. (*below*) Originally the old Chichester Theatre Southgate. In 1932 the headquarters of the County Library was situated behind the partition.

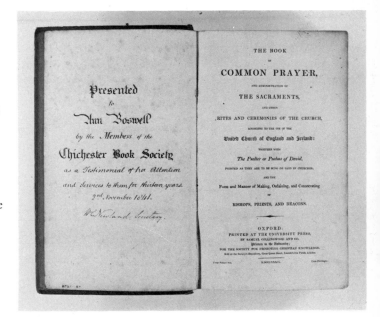

143. Yet another power cut in 1947 meant books by candlelight when the library was situated over the Butter Market.

144. The library moved to No. 22 West Street in May 1947.

145. The library in John Edes' house, then known as Wren House in West Street. It now houses the County Record Office.

146. (*above*) Chichester's first library van.

147 & 148. (*left & below*) Work begins on the removal of the book stock from above the Butter Market in North Street to 22 West Street, May 1947.

149. The opening of the new County Library headquarters in Tower Street, 1967. The ceremony of unlocking the door was performed by Professor Asa Briggs, under the approving eye of the Rev. Gordon Bearman, County Librarian.

150. Professor Briggs in company with Dr. Read, Director of Education.

151. This excellent photograph of the West Sussex County Library was taken from the cathedral bell tower.

152. The old Oliver Whitby School building, West Street, prior to rebuilding at the beginning of the century. The roof tablet reads: 'Charity-school founded by Oliver Whitby, Esq., A.D. 1702'. (See also *Bygone Chichester* Plates 104 & 105).

153. (*left*) Child's school slate discovered during excavations in Tower Street.

154. (*above*) Children of the Bishop Otter Infants' School, College Lane, c. 1895.

155. (*below*) Teacher and children at Portfield Infants' School, late 19th century.

156. Portfield School, May 1913.

157 & 158. The Barton Testimonial was the main prize of the Chichester Lancastrian Schools. The recipient of the prize in 1909 was Ethel Tester, future mother of the author.

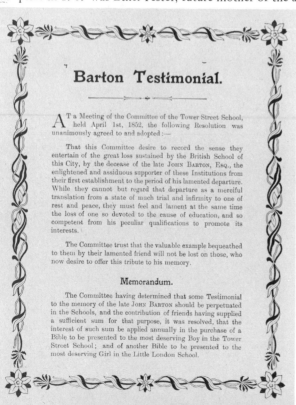

Barton Testimonial.

A T a Meeting of the Committee of the Tower Street School, held April 1st, 1852, the following Resolution was unanimously agreed to and adopted :—

That this Committee desire to record the sense they entertain of the great loss sustained by the British School of this City, by the decease of the late JOHN BARTON, Esq., the enlightened and assiduous supporter of these Institutions from their first establishment to the period of his lamented departure. While they cannot but regard that departure as a merciful translation from a state of much trial and infirmity to one of rest and peace, they must feel and lament at the same time the loss of one so devoted to the cause of education, and so competent from his peculiar qualifications to promote its interests.

The Committee trust that the valuable example bequeathed to them by their lamented friend will not be lost on those, who now desire to offer this tribute to his memory.

Memorandum.

The Committee having determined that some Testimonial to the memory of the late JOHN BARTON should be perpetuated in the Schools, and the contribution of friends having supplied a sufficient sum for that purpose, it was resolved, that the interest of such sum be applied annually in the purchase of a Bible to be presented to the most deserving Boy in the Tower Street School; and of another Bible to be presented to the most deserving Girl in the Little London School.

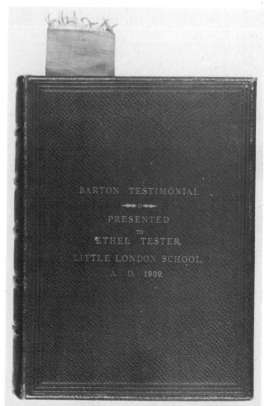

BARTON TESTIMONIAL

PRESENTED
TO
ETHEL TESTER,
LITTLE LONDON SCHOOL,
A. D. 1909.

59. (*top*) A rare classroom view
taken at the Central Boys School, New
Park Road, *c.* 1913.

60. (*above*) A more usual open-air group, Central Boys School,
. 1897. It is very rare to find the names of children recorded as
hey are here. Back row (*left to right*): Hutchings, Dean, Ralph,
arnett, Briant, Gilmore, Cousens, York; third row: Keys, Sivyer,
Hearn, Cooper, Batchelor, Elderton, Smart, Simmonds, Turner;
econd row: Horton, Dearling, Cumberlege, Wakeford, Mew,
apper, Wren, Carpenter; front row: Ticehurst, Wellcome,
ottrell, Caiger, Willard, Harper, Munt, Shippam.

61. (*right*) Directions printed in most excercise books
arlier in the century.

DIRECTIONS FOR THE PUPIL.

1.—Do not lean your chest against the desk.

2.—Keep your elbows off the desk.

3.—Do not sit sideways.

4.—Keep your shoulders square with the desk.

5.—Do not let your head hang forward.

6.—Keep two fingers on the pen.

7.—Do not hold your pen too close to the point.

8.—Keep both points of your pen on the paper.

9.—Let your penholder point to your right shoulder.

10.—Write slowly, and you will soon learn to write quickly and well.

162. St Margaret's High School, North Pallant, *c.* 1920. This rear view of the school shows the fine house that was eventually demolished adjoining Pallant House. The headmistress was Miss Billen; boys were taken to the age of 10, girls to 14; later the school moved to Pound Farm Road.

163. (*left*) School report for Walter Dew at Gordon School, No. 3 North Street.

164. (*below*) The school cap badge. The school took its name from Gordon House in the Hornet, where it had been founded by Miss Isabel Olden; later they moved to the North Street premises which Miss Olden shared with her sister who ran a wool and fancy goods business.

SCHOOL REPORT FORM.

GORDON SCHOOL.

NAME *Walter Dew*

CLASS *I*   No. of Scholars in Class

REPORT ON	*Easter Term* 192*8*
Reading	*Very Good*
Dictation	*Good*
Composition	*Good*
Writing	*Generally neat*
Arithmetic	*Absent from the*
Geography	*Exams. but progress*
History	*made through the*
English	*Terms work.*
Object Lesson	
Drawing	*Good*
~~Modelling~~ Scripture	*~~Absent~~ Good*
General Intelligence	*Very Good*
General Neatness	*Always neat in his work.*
Progress	*Good*
~~Needlework~~ Recitation	*Good*
Printing	*Good*
French	*Absent*

I. Olden

65. A bill for 12s. 9d. being a full terms tuition in 1909.

Mrs Hill
To I. Olden
Summer Term /09

Tuition to Master Hill   11 . 0
Use of bks & Stationery   1 . 0
Copied Exercise bks.   9
Settled   S. 12 . 9
Sept. 11 /09 I. Olden

School will re-open (D.V.)
on Tuesday, Sept. 7th /09.

166. Miss Olden's desk with attached seat.

167. Bishop Otter College weekend course for West Sussex teachers. Easter 1930.

168. A most elegantly posed group, reflecting Edwardian England, of Principal and staff, Bishop Otter College, 1908.

169. Senior class room, Bishop Otter College.

170. (*above left*) A printed list of the Corporation of the City of Chichester, 1796. The printer was Joseph Seagrave, one of the finest printers in England. His premises were at 21 East Street.

171. (*above right*) The original toll-board with list of tolls and bye-laws, on the opening of Chichester cattle market in 1871.

172. (*left*) Hunston windmill, a black smock mill built in 1720. It ceased work just over 200 years later and has since been demolished.

173. This most fascinating photograph depicts Runcton Manor with a game of croquet in progress on the lawn. *c.* 1870

174. (*below*) Sheep washing at Lavant.

175a. (*right*) Walter Grainger was a Fishbourne pig-farmer who lived in a caravan in a field at the rear of the *Black Boy*. Mr. Grainger, with his horse and cart, were very much part of the Chichester scene during World War II.

175. Fishbourne water-mill seen from the rear looking across the Mill Pond. 19th century.

176. Another view of Sadler's Mill.

177. The main road at Fishbourne soon after the turn of the century.

8. A few timbered piles and scattered bricks and masonry are all that remain of the salt mill in Fishbourne eek. Salt was produced here until 1840; it was then converted to a tide-mill for grain. Soon after 1906 it began fall into decay.

9. The old flour mill by the Fishbourne mill pond was destroyed by fire in 1918. Rebuilt, it finished commercial tivity in 1956, manufacturing macaroni. In 1958 it was converted into flats, giving fine views to the harbour.

180. Children at play in the early years of this century by Fishbourne mill pond.

181. The cathedral weathercock is brought down for repairs.

182. St James' Post, near Spitalfield Lane, was a regular seat for a Chichester character nicknamed 'Blind Harry'.

183. A Thomas Russell photograph of a proud Cicestrian with his penny farthing bicycle. *ca.* 1885.

184. Alderman Ebenezer Prior, a man of great influence in Chichester during the late 19th century. He was one of the leading wool buyers and merchants in the south of England.

185. This interesting photograph is titled 'Solid Sussex', and depicts the county's nine conservative members of parliament on the terrace of the House of Commons in 1887. Back row (*left to right*): Earl of March & Kinrara (South Western (Chichester)); Hon. A. E. Gathorn-Hardy (Northern (East Grinstead)); Admiral Field (Southern (Eastbourne)); Wilson Noble, Esq (Hastings); A. M. Brookfield, Esq (Eastern (Rye)). Front row (*left to right*) Sir Henry Fletcher, Bt (Mid (Lewes)); Col. Sir W. Barttelot, Bt. C.B. (North Western (Horsham)); Dr. Robertson (Brighton); Rt. Hon. W. Marriott, Q.C. (Brighton).

186. In 1923 Lloyd George spoke at Chichester cattle market in support of the local Liberal parliamentary candidate, helping to achieve an epic Liberal victory. A generation later Mr. Jo Grimond, then leader of the Liberal party, spoke just as eloquently, but did not achieve the same result.

187. Between the wars the British heavyweight boxing champion, Joe Beckett, trained at Chichester. Here he takes tea with the Mayor and Mayoress.

188. The Chichester Ladies Cricket XI.

189. Chichester's Special Constabulary, *ca.* 1918.

190. H.M. Queen Mary attracts a crowd of loyal citizens as she visits Chichester antique shops in 1929.

191. The White Rose Cricket Club of which Charlie Newell was a member in the summer of 1938. On the day that war was declared in 1939, they cycled to Hunston to play cricket against the village, with gas masks over their shoulders. Later, they became the White Rose Concert Party.

192. The 90th meeting of the 'Morris Ring'. A grand occasion for morris dancing and its supporters when 250 morris men from many parts of Britain came to Chichester in 1963. They are seen here dancing in the garden of the Bishop's Palace.

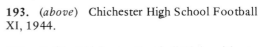

193. (*above*) Chichester High School Football XI, 1944.

194. (*left*) Chichester Football Club, with trophy, in Priory Park.

195. (*below left*) A rare photograph of Chichester Gasworks Football Club.

196. (*left*) Albert Sammons was Britain's leading violin soloist during the twenties and thirties. He was an outstanding musician and a great teacher. He lived locally and frequently performed in Bognor Regis and Chichester. His biography is now being written.

197. Miss Petula Clark, a star of international stature, who grew up in the Chichester area and has sung in the city many times. This photograph of her was taken by the author in 1959.

CHI·CHESTER
CONCERT

An Ode
written after hearing
Beethoven's Sonata, Opus 109
played at a pianoforte recital in
Chichester Cathedral

BY
MARTIN ARMSTRONG

CAMBRIDGE
At the University Press
1944

T. S. ELIOT, O.M., LL.D.

The Value and Use of Cathedrals
in England To-day

198 & 199. Two slim publications, ephemeral in their paper covers, but of permanent interest to all who love Chichester.

200. (*left*) Mr. Barry Cunliffe, the young Cambridge undergraduate, director of the excavation of the Fishbourne Roman Palace. He was later appointed Professor of Archaeology at Southampton University. Professor Cunliffe now has the Chair of European Archaeology at Oxford.

201. (*below*) Suddenly, residents of Fishbourne discovered that there was a palace at the bottom of their gardens. Excited visitors have the first glimpse of the 'Dolphin Mosaic' buried but a few inches below the surface for nearly 2,000 years.

HUNGARIAN RELIEF FUND

I appeal to all who enjoy and love freedom to help the refugees of Hungary.

This is nothing to do with the main international situation or party politics. It is just sheer humanity and I know everyone will be anxious to do their best to help.

I shall be at the Assembly Room, North Street, Chichester, on TUESDAY continuously from **5 p.m. till 10 p.m.** and I shall be delighted personally to receive your GIFTS, small or large, of **money, cheques and good warm clothing** to be sent to the Red Cross Organisation through the Lord Mayor of London's Relief Fund.

You are also invited to attend a

PUBLIC MEETING

in the Assembly Room that same evening (Tuesday) at 7 p.m.

L. EVERSHED-MARTIN,
Mayor of Chichester.

10th November, 1956.

202 & 203. (*above & above right*) In the winter of 1956, news of the Hungarian uprising and a flood of refugees caused consternation throughout the world. The citizens of Chichester were swift in response to the Mayor's appeal.

204 & 205. (*right*) The St John Ambulance Brigade have always been strong in Chichester, and their presence at most public events has made them many friends. Here we see the dedication and handing over of ambulances at the Bishop's Palace, by Bishop Southwell.

PROGRAMME

1. OMBRA MAI FU (XERXES)
   THE ENEMY SAID (ISRAEL IN EGYPT)
   SILENT WORSHIP (PTOLEMY)   } *Handel*
   SOUND AN ALARM (JUDAS MACCABAEUS)

   HEDDLE NASH

2. PRELUDE AND FUGUE IN A MINOR   *Bach-Liszt*

   HARRIET COHEN

3. O RAVISHING DELIGHT   *Arne*
   WITH THEE THE UNSHELTERED MOOR I'D TREAD
   (SOLOMON)   *Handel*
   O HAD I JUBAL'S LYRE (JOSHUA)   *Handel*

   ISOBEL BAILLIE

   ::::::::::::::::::
   SHORT INTERVAL
   ::::::::::::::::::

4. MY LOVELY CELIA   *Arr. Lane Wilson*
   THE PASSIONATE SHEPHERD   *Peter Warlock*
   SO SWEET IS SHEE   *Arr. Arnold Dolmetsch*
   IT WAS A LOVER AND HIS LASS   *Barbara Reynolds*
   WINTER   *Balfour Gardiner*

   HEDDLE NASH

5. TWO ETUDES   *Chopin*
   TWO SPANISH DANCES   *De Falla*

   HARRIET COHEN

6. TWILIGHT FANCIES   *Delius*
   FAERY SONG (THE IMMORTAL HOUR)   *Rutland Boughton*
   IF MY SONGS WERE ONLY WINGED   *Hahn*
   SERENADE   *Richard Strauss*

   ISOBEL BAILLIE

7. SCENE FROM THE 1st ACT OF LA BOHEME   *Puccini*

   YOUR TINY HAND IS FROZEN

   HEDDLE NASH

   MIMI'S SONG

   ISOBEL BAILLIE

   LOVELY MAID IN THE MOONLIGHT

   ISOBEL BAILLIE AND HEDDLE NASH

   ::::::::::::::::::

   GOD SAVE THE KING

STEINWAY CONCERT GRAND PIANOFORTE BY STORRY'S

206. (*above*) The Chichester Girl's Club dinner at Kimbell's, North Street. *ca*.1950.

207. (*left*) The Plaza Theatre, later the Odeon cinema, in South Street, presented many fine concert programmes during the 1940s. This programme is typical of such events.

208. (*above*) The Right Worshipful, the Mayor of Chichester, Charles Newell, together with the Mayoress, entertain Bishop and Mrs. Wilson to tea following the enthronement ceremony, 25 April, 1958.

209. (*right*) Bishop Roger Wilson leaves the Bishop's Palace for the west door of the cathedral and his enthronement as Bishop of Chichester.

210. (*left*) The young Charlie Newell, whose career took him from bloater boy at Shippam's to Mayor and Freeman of the City of Chichester.

211. (*below*) Charlie Newell was to give much of his life to the welfare of the elderly. The Newell Centre in St Pancras bears testimony to his labours. This photograph shows the first old age pensioner's party, given by himself, in 1946.

212. The Mayor and Mayoress at a reception for Bishop Bell on 23 January 1958. Mrs. Bell is also present.

213. At the opening of the St John Ambulance headquarters, 11 April 1958.

214. The Mayor presents the Freedom of the City to Aldermen Mr. and Mrs. Eastland, 22 January 1959.

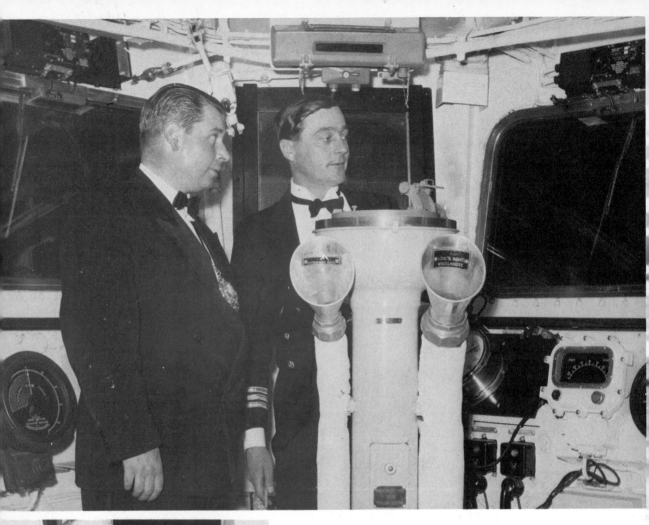

215. (*above*) The Mayor aboard HMS Chichester, June 1958.

216 (*left*) The Mayors of the cities of Chartres and Chichester, sign the twinning document that binds their cities in friendship.

217. (*below*) Bronze and silver medals presented to the Mayor of Chichester by the city of Chartres.

218. (*above*) From this unlikely beginning in March 1956, Charlie and Marjorie Newell set about the creation of a day centre for the elderly in the Hornet.

219. (*right*) It was slow work and much of it was done themselves, but the Newell family had never held back when effort was required.

220. (*below*) The day centre ready for use. Now the Newell Centre in St Pancras has become the focal point for senior citizens in the area.

CHICHESTER JAZZ CLUB
Bull's Head Inn, Fishbourne

The Club will be open during the Summer every Friday, as well as Tuesdays, commencing with

THE TUBBY HAYES ORCHESTRA

on **Friday 24 May**, 8 p.m.—Midnight

This is the debut of Tubby's new 13 piece orchestra, its first appearance anywhere in Gt. Britain, and will be covered by the national musical press

Tubby Hayes   *Tenor, Flute and Vibraphone*
Jimmie Deuchar · Les Condon · Ian Hamer   *Trumpets*
Ken Wray · Keith Christie   *Trombones*
Johnny Laine · Peter King   *Saxes*
Stan Robinson · Jackie Sharpe   *Saxes*
Terry Shannon *Piano* Freddie Logan *Bass* Alan Ganley *Drums*

Admission by Ticket only   Limited Number **10/- each**

Tickets from : Jazz Club, Tuesdays
or Bull's Head Inn, on any day during opening hours
or By post from the Secretary, Chichester Jazz Club,
Bull's Head Inn, Fishbourne, Chichester, Sussex.
(Postal Orders, please, and S.A.E.)

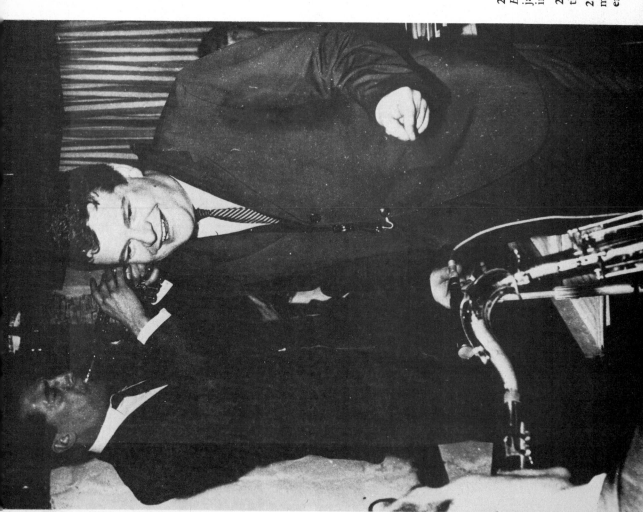

221. (*left*)   The Chichester Jazz Club founded by Don Norman at the *Bull's Head* Inn, Fishbourne, was to become a major centre for modern jazz. Seen here is the late Tubby Hayes, a brilliant jazz musician and instrumentalist whose work is now legendary.

222. (*above*)   During the early 1960s the club enjoyed its heyday, as this poster shows.

223. (*below*)   A session in full swing, with Tubby Hayes and his band making the rafters ring. There were some complaints from local residents about noise.

224.   Sand yachts racing at Bracklesham Bay. This was a popular sport with a number of Chichester people between the wars. A particular enthusiast was Sir Malcolm Campbell who frequently brought his young son, Donald, as crew.

225.   The Goodwood Motoring Festival, 14 July 1962. Donald Campbell (left) with his father's 1920 350 h.p. Sunbeam. Leo Villa, who was engineer for both the Campbells stands by the rebuilt *Bluebird*.

226. (*right*) Sir Henry Royce described himself simply as a mechanic. He is undoubtedly among the great engineers of the world. From 1917 until his death in 1933 he lived and worked in the village of West Wittering, at Elmstead in Elm Lane. Here we see Sir Henry at Elmstead at the wheel of an experimental car, a 40/50 *Silver Ghost* with a prototype 'New Phantom' engine installed, *c.* 1923.

227. (*centre*) Sir Henry and his engineering and design staff celebrate the Schneider Trophy victory in his garden at Elmstead. (See introduction).

228. One of the two Supermarine S6B Schneider Trophy aircraft of 1931, powered by the Rolls-Royce 'R' engine. The Supermarine S6 was designed by R. T. Mitchell who later designed the Spitfire; Sir Henry's contribution was the Merlin Aero engine.

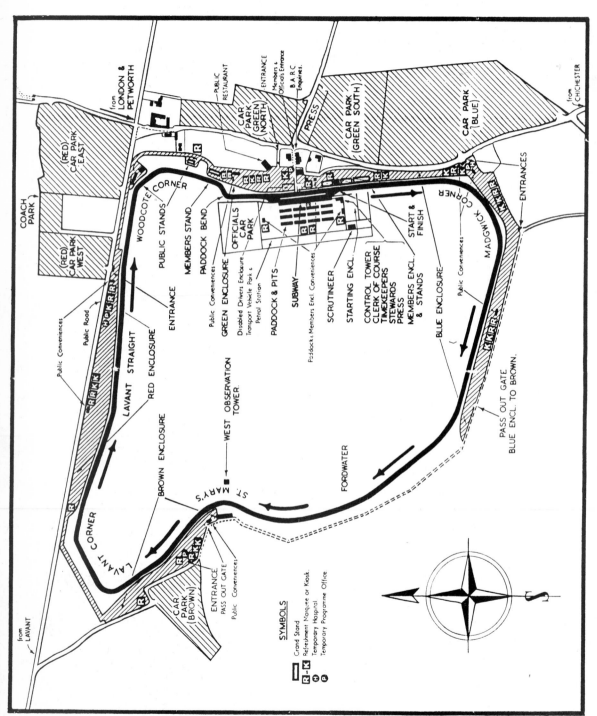

229. Plan of the Goodwood motor circuit, developed from the West Hampnett wartime airfield that was a satellite to Tangmere.

230. The start of the Goodwood International '100' for Formula 1 cars, April 1961. On the front row (*left to right*): Stirling Moss, John Surtees, Roy Salvadori and Graham Hill. Behind Moss is Innes Ireland.

231. Squadron Leader Neville Duke, at the controls of his Hawker Hunter, powered by a Rolls-Royce Avon engine, during his record breaking flights over Chichester and West Sussex in September 1953.

232. Three years later, Peter Twiss piloted Fairey Delta 2 between Chichester and Ford and broke the world air-speed record by 310 mph. The FD2 was designed and used as a research aircraft to investigate the problems of high speed flight. This aircraft was the precursor to the Concorde with its droop-nose and delta wings.

233. Peter Twiss reached a speed of 1,132 mph. and was the last Briton to hold the record. The record was achieved under great secrecy, supersonic bangs were constantly complained of. Timing devices and cameras were set up at the Chichester sewage works at Apuldram by a team from Farnborough.

1132

MILES PER HOUR

10ᵀᴴ MARCH 1956

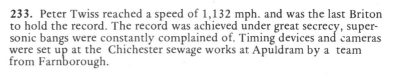

234. Success!

235. Looking back on it all over a glass of sherry.

236. (right) The Very Rev. Dean Hannah dedicates Chichester's War Memorial.

237. Field Marshal Sir William Robertson at the unveiling ceremony, 20 July 1921.

238. The vast crowd reaches far into the Hornet.

239 & 240. Older Cicestrians will well recall the services held in Eastgate Square. Here, the Right Worshipful Mayor of Chichester, Alderman Walter Stride, and the Mayoress, lead the City Council and the people of Chichester on Remembrance Day. They received the Freedom of Chichester following their leadership during World War II. Also seen here is the Very Rev. Dean Duncan-Jones.

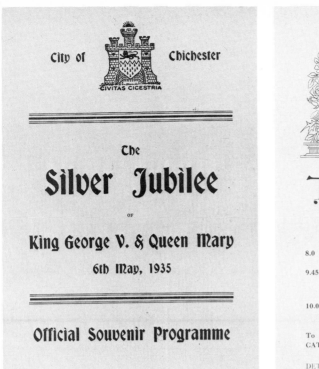

City of Chichester

CIVITAS CICESTRIA

The

Silver Jubilee

OF

King George V. & Queen Mary

6th May, 1935

Official Souvenir Programme

1910 · 1935

THE SILVER JUBILEE WILL BE CELEBRATED IN THE CITY ON THE 6th MAY, 1935, WHEN THE FOLLOWING

PROGRAMME

WILL BE CARRIED OUT.

8.0 a.m. There will be a ROYAL SALUTE OF TWENTY-FIVE GUNS.

9.45 a.m. THE MAYOR AND CORPORATION will assemble in the COUNCIL CHAMBER, and proceed to the RECREATION GROUND, in New Park Road, where at

10.0 a.m. There will assemble to form

A PROCESSION

To THE SPECIAL THANKSGIVING SERVICE in the CATHEDRAL, at 11.0 a.m., in the subjoining order:
CHICHESTER CITY BAND
DETACHMENT OF THE 4th BATTALION ROYAL SUSSEX REGIMENT

241 & 242. Part of the souvenir programme for the Silver Jubilee of King George V and Queen Mary.

243. The proclamation at the City Cross of King Edward VIII in January 1936.

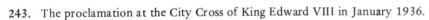

CORONATION

of their Majesties

King George VI. & Queen Elizabeth

Wednesday, May 12th, 1937

CITY OF CHICHESTER

Official Programme of Festivities - 6d.

To

Celebrate the Coronation

———— Of Their Majesties ————

On WEDNESDAY, 12th MAY, 1937
THE CITIZENS OF CHICHESTER
will unite in the following Programme
of Festivities

•

God Bless Their Majesties

CITY OF CHICHESTER CORONATION PROGRAMME

4.15 p.m.—

THE CHILDREN WILL ASSEMBLE FOR
TEA

and each Child will be presented with a Coronation Mug

One verse of "**God Save The King**" will be sung, followed by Grace (Tune—"Old Hundredth"):—

*Be present at our Table, Lord;
Be here and everywhere adored;
Bless these Thy gifts and grant that we
May feast in Paradise with Thee. Amen.*

After Tea, a **CORONATION MEDAL**, the personal gift of the Mayor and Mayoress, will be presented to each child.

Grace will then be sung (Tune, "Old Hundredth"):—

*We thank Thee, Lord, for this our food
For life and health and every good;
May Manna to our Souls be given,
The Bread of life sent down from Heaven. Amen.*

4.45 p.m. — THE PRIORY PARK WILL BE OPENED TO PARENTS.

All children must leave the Park by 7 p.m.

N.B.—In the event of inclement weather, **THREE MAROONS** will be fired at 12.30 p.m. to indicate that the alternative programme (details of which have been arranged), will be substituted for the programme in Priory Park.

KING GEORGE VI. & QUEEN ELIZABETH — 1937

244, 245 & 246. Part of the Chichester programme for the Coronation celebration of King George VI and Queen Elizabeth, 12 May 1937.

247 & 248. (*above left & right*) The Right
Worshipful Mayor of Chichester, Councillor
Russell Purchase proclaims to the people of
Chichester, in the traditional manner, the
succession to the throne of Her Majesty,
Queen Elizabeth II, 1952.

249. (*right*) As Coronation Day 1953 drew
near, millions of people throughout Britain
demonstrated their loyalty by decorating
their homes. One such person was Mrs. May
Cooper seen here at the door of her cottage
in Tower Street, now demolished.

250. (*right*) Mr. Basil Shippam was a staunch friend and benefactor of the city. In this photograph he signs the Roll of Honorary Freeman of Chichester.

251. (*right*) A military band marches through Chichester on an early Gala Day morning.

252. Decorations for a royal visit. When Her Majesty the Queen came to Chichester in 1956, was the first official visit by a sovereign to Chichester for 50 years.

253 & 254. Queen Elizabeth is met by the Duke of Norfolk as she arrives in Chichester's Priory Park. Waiting to greet her is the Right Worshipful Mayor of Chichester, Councillor Leslie Evershed-Martin, together with his wife Carol, the Mayoress, and the Town Clerk, Mr. Eric Banks.

255 & 256. Queen Elizabeth is quickly joined by the Duke of Edinburgh: Her Majesty is invited to inspect a Guard of Honour formed by men of the Royal Sussex Regiment.

257. The city councillors come forward individually to meet the Queen.

258 As with all royal visits, the programme was packed with engagements. The first visit was to the 13th-century Guildhall.

259 & 260. (*left & below left*) The Royal visitors went on to visit the cathedral, and St Mary's Hospital in St Martin's Square. Thousands of people had an opportunity to cheer them as they made their way by car about the city.

261. Four very lucky young people about to meet their Queen in Priory Park

62. Leslie Evershed-Martin developed the idea of building a theatre in Chichester in January 1959. In 1962 it opened s doors to its first public audience as the Chichester Festival Theatre, with Sir Laurence Olivier as its first director. It as built just outside the city walls in the beautiful setting of Oaklands Park.

63. On 12 May 1961, Her Royal Highness Princess lexandra of Kent came to Chichester to lay the found- ion stone of the theatre. The Princess shakes hands with ohn Neville who spoke a twelve line sonnet composed by r. Christopher Fry. Mr. Fry is standing on Mr. Neville's ght.

264. Her Royal Highness declares the stone well and truly laid.

265. (*left*) The advice and experience of Sir Tyrone Guthrie was of enormous help in the early days of the theatre. Here he is interviewed for television by Roy Rich (*left*).

266. (*centre*) The concrete and cantilever constru tion surrounded by a mass of scaffolding steadily begins to take shape.

267. (*below*) The 'topping out' with beer all roun as Sir Laurence Olivier thanks the workforce for the great efforts.

268 & 269. (*opposite above & below*) Sir Lauren Olivier casts an eye over the completed theatre and its surroundings, and the great actor steps on to the thrust stage that he will bring to life with characters from Shakespeare to Chekhov.

270. (*above*) The Queen Mother arrives at the Festival Theatre for the gala performance of 'Love's Labour's Lost'. It was performed by the Stratford (Ontario) Festival Company of Canada.

271. (*left*) Her Majesty finds time to talk with young people from St John Ambulance Brigade.

272. A wooden jig-saw puzzle that is both interesting and unusual, *c.* 1925. For many people its appearance will also personify the impact and inroads that demolition has brought to so many parts of Chichester.

273. There has always been an interest in swimming in Chichester. This enthusiasm crystallised in the city in 1957 when Mr. Ronnie Edgar founded the Cormorant Swimming Club. This photograph of the club was taken in 1958.

274. It was not long before the 'Cormorants' began to generate public interest for a swimming pool in Chichester. This picture shows a gala procession entry with all types of bath from hip to blanket! David Daughtry, then captain of the 'Cormorants', stands on the lorry far left.

275 & 276. (*above & above right*) When the Gaumont cinema closed its doors, fund raising began in an effort to achieve a much needed pool. Soon the gutted cinema began to take shape as a pool and the results were spectacular. Between 1968 and 1980 an average of 1,800 pupils per week attended the pool with their schools.

277 & 278. (*centre & below*) Chichester's swimming pool was officially opened by His Grace the Duke of Richmond and Gordon, on 29 April 1967, and as the pictures show, a good time was had by all.

ACKNOWLEDGEMENTS

While many of the photographs that appear in this book are from my own collection, I wish to thank all those people who have so readily responded to my requests for additional material. I am particularly grateful for all the help given me by the people and organisations named below:

British Aerospace; Miss Angela Bell; Mr. George Bevis; Mr. Graham Brooks; Mr. Peter Benham; Mr. Peter Burnand; Mr. R. H. Briggs; Miss Lillian Birtill; The National Motor Museum, Beaulieu; Mr. Jack de Coninck; Mr. Michael Coviello; Sqn-Ldr Neville Duke; Mr. Walter Dew; Mr. and Mrs. David Daughtry; The photographs of Sir Laurence Olivier are reproduced by kind permission of Epoque Ltd.; Mr. and Mrs. J. O. Edwards; Mr. Michael Evans; Mr. Christopher Fry; Mrs. Eileen Gordon; Miss Anne Hillier; Mr. Alec H. Hill; Mr. Philip Harris; Messrs. Howard & Son, Photographers; Mr. R. Harmer; Mrs. Izard; The Rev. F. J. Jackson; Mr. Alec Lumsden; Mr. L. Evershed-Martin; Mr. and Mrs. V. Meynell; The Meynell Collection; Mr. Richard Meynell; Sir Robert McAlpine & Sons Ltd. of London; Mr. and Mrs. Charlie Newell; Mr. Don Norman; The Portsmouth and Sunderland Newspaper Group; Associated Newspaper Group Ltd.; Mr. Noel Osborne; Chichester Photographic Service; Mr. Hugh Palmer; Messrs. Rolls-Royce Ltd.; Messrs. C. Shippam Ltd.; Mr. Philip Scott; Mrs. C. M. Scutt; Mr. Victor Slaymaker; Mr. Michael Stroud; Mr. Peter Twiss; The Rev. R. Thomas; West Sussex County Planning Dept.; West Sussex Institute of Higher Education; The West Sussex County Library Service; Mr. Trevor York.